A BOOK ABOUT

# ANXIETY

HEALTHY **MINDS**

BY

## HOLLY DUHIG

**PowerKiDS** press™

Published in 2020 by The Rosen
Publishing Group, Inc.
29 East 21st Street, New York, NY 10010

Cataloging-in-Publication Data
Names: Duhig, Holly.
Title: A book about anxiety / Holly Duhig.
Description: New York : PowerKids Press, 2020. | Series: Healthy minds
| Includes glossary and index.
Identifiers: ISBN 9781725314603 (pbk.) | ISBN 9781725314627 (library bound)
| ISBN 9781725314610 (6 pack)
Subjects: LCSH: Anxiety disorders--Juvenile literature.
Classification: LCC RC531.D84 2020 | DDC 616.85'22--dc23

This edition is published by arrangement with Booklife Publishing

Written by: Holly Duhig
Edited by: Kirsty Holmes
Designed by: Danielle Jones

## PHOTOCREDITS

Front Cover – Elena Elisseeva. 4 – Monkey Business Images, goodluz. 5 – Monkey Business Images, pathdoc. 6 – Bukavik, Jan H Andersen. 7 – Bukavik. 8 – FotoDuets. 9 – Bukavik, Kateryna Kon. 10 – EhayDy, daseugen, kryzhov. 11 – tommaso79, Sergey Novikov. 12 – PT Images, Photographee. eu. 13 – Christine Bird, estherpoon. 14 – ArtOfPhotos, Lindsay Helms, Olimpik. 15 – Kamira, Antonio Guillem. 16 – Africa Studio, Prostock-studio. 17 – lukpedclub, Bukavik. 18 – NattapolStudiO, Roman Bodnarchuk. 19 – SnowWhiteimages, Dmytro Zinkevych, David Franklin. 20 – Sk.Group_Studio. 21 – Africa Studio, XiXinXing. 22 – Andrey_Kuzmin, John D Sirlin. 23 – Mastaco, Monkey Business Images. 24 – asife, Photographee.eu. 25 – AJR_photo, ALPA PROD, asife. 26–27 – Bukavik. 28 – mypokcik, Monkey Business Images. 29 – Chuck Rausin , Prostock-studio. 30 – CREATISTA, Andrey_Popov. Images are courtesy of Shutterstock.com, unless stated otherwise. With thanks to Getty Images, Thinkstock Photo and iStockphoto.

Manufactured in the United States of America

CPSIA Compliance Information: Batch #CW20PK: For Further Information contact Rosen Publishing, New York, New York at 1-800-237-9932.

# CONTENTS

Words that look like **THIS** are explained in the glossary on page 31.

# WHAT IS ANXIETY?

Anxiety is the word we use to describe the feelings of fear and worry that we all experience from time to time. Many of us feel anxious on the first day of a new school year or when we have to take a test. Our thoughts might race and we might feel like there are knots in our stomach. These feelings are normal and can sometimes even be helpful because they let us know that what we are doing is important to us.

If someone feels highly anxious all the time, it can start to affect their day-to-day life and relationships, both with themselves and other people. This can be a sign of an anxiety disorder. An anxiety disorder is a mental health condition, which means it affects your mind, thoughts, and feelings. There are many types of anxiety disorders, but one of the most common is called generalized anxiety disorder or GAD.

BEING ANXIOUS BEFORE A BIG SPORTS MATCH CAN HELP GIVE YOU THE ENERGY YOU NEED TO PERFORM AT YOUR BEST.

Both children and adults can have mental health conditions like anxiety. Often mental health conditions are diagnosed by a doctor or **THERAPIST**. For people with a mental health condition like generalized anxiety disorder, high levels of anxiety can stop them from doing the things they enjoy as well as the things they need to do in their daily lives, like school or work.

Anxiety is a powerful emotion that affects our bodies as well as our minds. Some people's anxiety causes them to worry about lots of different things, whereas other people might worry about one particular thing. When you have anxiety, it can feel like there are lots of worries and fears taking up space in your mind. This can be very tiring and can make it difficult to concentrate on things like schoolwork or even fun things like spending time with friends, playing games, and reading books.

RESEARCH SUGGESTS THAT 3.1% OF PEOPLE IN THE U.S. HAVE GENERALIZED ANXIETY DISORDER.

# ANXIETY

Anxiety affects people in many ways, both **PHYSICALLY** and emotionally. This means that anxiety can have a noticeable effect on your body. Think back to a time where you felt scared. You might have had a racing heart, shaky legs, or a stomachache. Perhaps you felt too warm or short of breath. You might even have felt like crying or screaming. These are all **SYMPTOMS** of anxiety that happen in our bodies.

Physical symptoms of anxiety can cause us to worry even more because they make us believe there is something wrong with us, or that we are ill. It is important to remember that, as uncomfortable and scary as these symptoms can be, they can't hurt you and they will go away when you feel calm again. Some of the physical symptoms of anxiety are:

BLURRED VISION

HEADACHE

DIFFICULTY SWALLOWING

FEELING SICK

RACING HEART OR **PALPITATIONS**

STOMACHACHE

QUICK BREATHING

SWEATY HANDS

JELLY LEGS

## The Worry Cycle

When we are anxious, we tend to pay more attention to our bodies and how they feel. This can spark a cycle of worry and make feelings like **NAUSEA**, quick breathing, palpitations, and stomachaches seem more powerful than they actually are. Usually these feelings go away once we are calm again.

A WORRYING THOUGHT POPS INTO YOUR HEAD AND MAKES YOU FEEL ANXIOUS.

I'm not feeling very well. What if I throw up in front of everybody?

I really am going to be sick!

My stomach feels bad.

YOU THINK YOUR WORRIES MUST BE TRUE, WHICH CAUSES YOU TO WORRY EVEN MORE.

FEELINGS OF ANXIETY AFFECT YOUR BODY.

7

# ANXIETY AND THE BODY

Many scientists think that anxiety is caused by **CHEMICAL IMBALANCES** in the brain. Research has shown that people with anxiety sometimes have less of a chemical called serotonin in their brains. Serotonin is a chemical that helps to send messages between brain cells and helps keep your mood stable. When there isn't enough of this chemical, it can cause people to become more sad or anxious. Some people with anxiety are prescribed medication to help boost the levels of serotonin found between individual brain cells.

Dealing with anxiety can be difficult, but it can be easier when you understand what is happening inside your brain. The emotion of anxiety begins in the amygdala (say: a-MIG-duh-luh), which are two almond-shaped parts of the brain that are responsible for warning you about danger. They are part of the limbic system – the system in the brain that deals with our emotions. The amygdala tells the hypothalamus, another part of the brain, to react to worry and **STRESS**.

HYPOTHALAMUS

10% OF TEENAGERS AND 40% OF ADULTS SUFFER FROM AN ANXIETY DISORDER OF SOME KIND.

AMYGDALA

PEOPLE WITH AN ANXIETY DISORDER ARE THOUGHT TO HAVE AN OVERACTIVE AMYGDALA.

# Fight, Flight, Freeze

Your hypothalamus begins something called the fight, flight, freeze response in your body. This is the full-body response that gives you the energy to either face your fears (fight) or run away from them (flight). The third response, freeze, can happen when we feel so overwhelmed that we feel like we can't move or are stuck to the spot.

The hypothalamus sends a message to two **GLANDS** that sit above your kidneys, called your adrenal glands, telling them to release a **HORMONE** called adrenaline (sometimes called epinephrine).

These hormones tell certain parts of your body—such as your heart, lungs, and muscles—to work harder so that you can fight, or run away from, the thing that is frightening you.

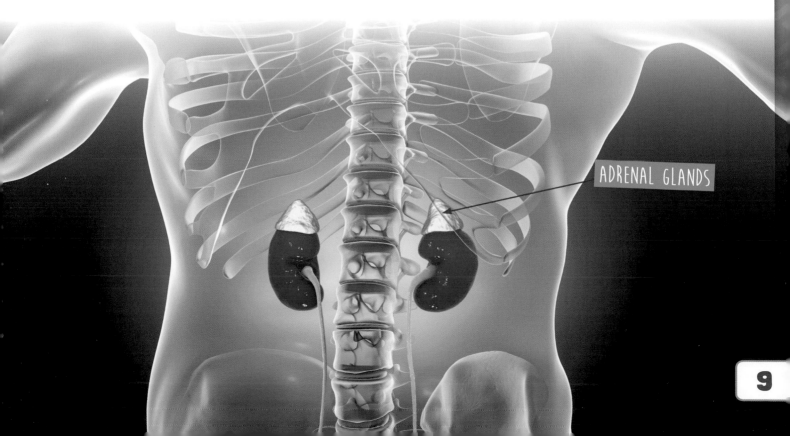

ADRENAL GLANDS

9

# WHY DO WE NEED FIGHT, FLIGHT, FREEZE?

Scientists think humans have developed the fight, flight, freeze response to fear because our **ANCESTORS** needed to fight and run away from dangerous predators. The freeze response may have even helped them to play dead or stay still long enough that a predator wouldn't notice them.

Nowadays, the things that frighten us aren't always life-and-death situations, and are often more complicated than that. For example, we might be scared of embarrassing ourselves in front of our friends, or we might be scared of failing a test. Humans are social animals, meaning that we work best when we live and work in large groups with many people. We might have **EVOLVED** to be scared of doing things wrong in front of others because, in the past, it would have helped our ancestors to stay part of their tribe.

SCIENTISTS THINK THE REASON SOME HUMANS ARE SCARED OF THE DARK IS BECAUSE OUR ANCESTORS WERE MORE LIKELY TO BE ATTACKED BY PREDATORS IN THE DARK.

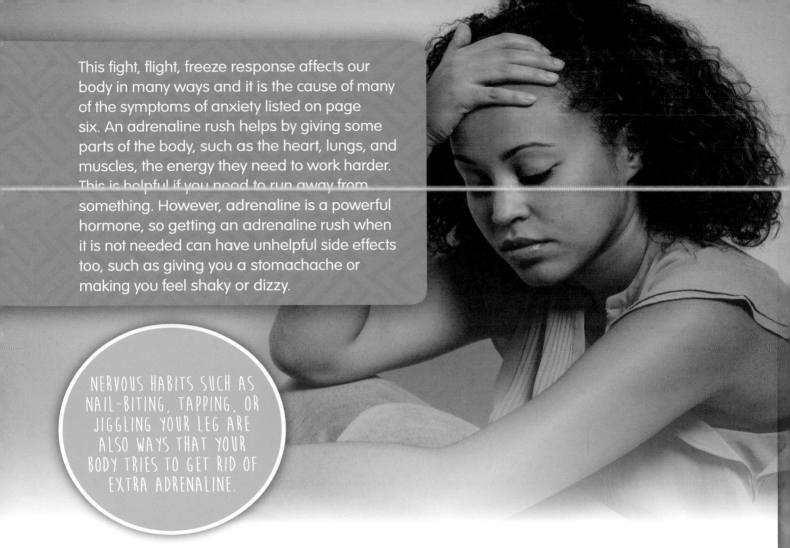

This fight, flight, freeze response affects our body in many ways and it is the cause of many of the symptoms of anxiety listed on page six. An adrenaline rush helps by giving some parts of the body, such as the heart, lungs, and muscles, the energy they need to work harder. This is helpful if you need to run away from something. However, adrenaline is a powerful hormone, so getting an adrenaline rush when it is not needed can have unhelpful side effects too, such as giving you a stomachache or making you feel shaky or dizzy.

NERVOUS HABITS SUCH AS NAIL-BITING, TAPPING, OR JIGGLING YOUR LEG ARE ALSO WAYS THAT YOUR BODY TRIES TO GET RID OF EXTRA ADRENALINE.

Some people with anxiety find that doing something active, like going for a run, swimming, or playing a sport, can help them feel calmer. Exercise helps with anxiety because it uses up the extra energy that an adrenaline rush causes.

# OTHER ANXIETY DISORDERS

As well as generalized anxiety disorder, there are many other types of anxiety disorders. Social anxiety disorder is a type of anxiety disorder that causes people to have an overwhelming fear about social situations. People with social anxiety often have difficulty talking to strangers or people they don't know very well. They might always be worried about doing something embarrassing in front of others and they might avoid group conversations, eating around others, or going to social events like parties. People with social anxiety disorder tend to have low **SELF-ESTEEM**, which means they don't feel very good about themselves. Social anxiety can make people feel very lonely.

Luckily, there are many ways to treat social anxiety and, like all types of anxiety, people can get better from it. Building confidence one step at a time with the help of a doctor or therapist can help people with this disorder to gain more confidence and become less anxious.

# Phobias

A phobia is a strong fear about one particular thing. Many people have fears of things such as snakes, spiders, needles, or heights. This is quite common. However, most of these fears are manageable and do not tend to affect people's lives too much. A phobia is different. It is an extremely strong fear that doesn't go away. People with phobias often try to avoid places or situations where they might come into contact with the thing that scares them. This can stop them from doing all the things they would like to do.

Agoraphobia (say: a-guh-ruh-FO-bee-uh) is a phobia that causes people to worry about being in crowded places such as football games, assemblies, or busy shopping centers, and not being able to leave easily. They might be afraid of having a panic attack in a crowded place and will tend to avoid situations where it is difficult to leave.

# MORE PHOBIAS

Claustrophobia (say: closs-truh-FO-bee-ah) is a fear of being in small spaces that you can't easily get out of. This might be elevators, tunnels, or public transportation like buses or trains.

Cynaphobia (say: sin-a-FO-bee-uh) is the fear of dogs. Many phobias are animal-related and dogs are a common phobia. People with cynaphobia may have had a bad experience with a dog in the past that caused them to have this fear.

Phobias are often treated with talk therapy, where a therapist will help someone with a phobia to better understand their fear. They might also help people gradually face up to their fears, but won't push them to do anything they are not ready for.

AROUND 5% OF CHILDREN AND 16% OF TEENAGERS WILL HAVE A SPECIFIC PHOBIA AT SOME POINT IN THEIR LIFETIME.

# Panic Disorder

Panic disorder is a type of anxiety disorder in which people experience **FREQUENT** panic attacks. A panic attack is a very **INTENSE** feeling of anxiety, fear, and discomfort that comes on suddenly. People who are experiencing a panic attack might:

- Have a racing heart and feel lightheaded
- Worry that they are going to die
- Feel like shouting or crying
- Feel out of control of their body

Panic disorder is often described as a **VICIOUS CYCLE** because people who have experienced a panic attack might worry that they are going to have another one. This leads to more anxiety, which leads to more panic attacks. They may even avoid the places or situations they were in when they last had a panic attack.

Panic attacks can be scary, but they can't hurt you and they only last for a short amount of time. Learning this can be the first step in overcoming panic disorder.

HAVING SOMEONE SIT WITH YOU AND HELP YOU CALM DOWN CAN HELP STOP A PANIC ATTACK.

# PANIC ATTACKS

Panic attacks can happen to anybody, not just people with a panic disorder. Panic attacks sometimes happen when you are in a place or situation that makes you anxious. For instance, if you are scared of being in crowded places, then busy shopping centers might be a **TRIGGER** for a panic attack. However, panic attacks can also happen without warning. Many children and adults experience them when they are at home relaxing.

If you experience panic attacks, being aware of what triggers them can help you to deal with them. For example, if every time you had a panic attack you were on vacation, it could help you realize that staying away from home is a trigger. Instead of avoiding these situations, talking to someone about what you are frightened of and learning new ways of staying calm (see page 20) can help you to feel better.

IT MAY HELP TO WRITE DOWN WHERE YOU WERE AND WHAT YOU WERE DOING WHEN YOU HAD A PANIC ATTACK.

# Calming Down

## Sensory Grounding

You can think of panic attacks like fire drills. Sometimes fire alarms need to be tested to make sure they are still working. In the same way, the body needs to test our fight, flight, freeze responses. These tests just tend to happen more often for people with anxiety. Luckily, there are many ways to calm down from a panic attack. Sensory grounding is just one of those ways. Sensory grounding is all about using your senses to relax and become aware of your surroundings.

## STEP 1:
START BY TAKING SLOW, DEEP BREATHS. BREATHE IN FOR THE COUNT OF FOUR AND OUT FOR SIX.

## STEP 2:
LOOK AROUND YOU. CAN YOU LIST FIVE THINGS THAT YOU CAN SEE? CAN YOU SEE PEOPLE AROUND YOU? WHAT COLOR IS THE FLOOR?

## STEP 4:
PAY ATTENTION TO YOUR BODY. CAN YOU LIST THREE THINGS YOU CAN FEEL? PERHAPS YOU CAN FEEL YOUR CLOTHES ON YOUR SKIN. WHERE ARE YOU SITTING? CAN YOU FEEL THE FURNITURE?

## STEP 3:
LISTEN UP. CAN YOU LIST FOUR THINGS YOU CAN HEAR? IT MIGHT BE PEOPLE TALKING, OR CARS DRIVING OUTSIDE.

My name is Omar and I get anxious about lots of things. Waking up for school makes me really anxious because I am always thinking about all the things that could go wrong during the day. I don't like sitting in the classroom or the assembly hall because it feels like everyone is watching me and I feel trapped. I get scared that I'll do something embarrassing in front of all my friends like cry or panic. My worries get even worse when we have a test or do silent reading because I know I definitely can't leave the classroom without getting in trouble.

One day I knew I had to present my geography project to my class after lunch and I had been worried about it all day. My stomach was turning over and I couldn't eat any food because I was just too scared, so I decided to hide somewhere in the playground instead of going back inside after lunch.

My teacher noticed I was missing and came to find me. She was angry at first because she thought I was skipping class, but when I told her I was scared, she was kind and helped me calm down. Since then, I have been seeing a counselor for anxiety. My counselor is really good at making the things I am worried about feel less frightening. I go to see him once a week and he gives me lots of methods to use when I need to calm down.

TIME OUT

My teacher also gave me a time-out card that I can show her if I am too anxious and need to leave the classroom. Just knowing I can leave if I need to makes me feel so much better, so I haven't actually used it that often. Still, it's nice to know that it's there if I really need it. I think it might take a long time for my anxiety to go away completely, but with the help of my counselor it has already become much easier to deal with.

# RELAXATION TECHNIQUES

Relaxation techniques are methods that anyone can use to calm down when they feel anxious. One of these techniques is called progressive muscle relaxation. This is where you relax the different muscles in your body one at a time. Here's how to do it:

## STEP 1:

STARTING WITH YOUR FEET, SQUEEZE THE MUSCLES IN YOUR TOES AS YOU INHALE (BREATHE IN) AND RELAX THEM WHEN YOU EXHALE (BREATHE OUT). TRY TO BREATHE IN FOR A COUNT OF FOUR AND OUT FOR A COUNT OF SIX. IF YOU RELAX YOUR BODY, YOUR MIND WILL FOLLOW.

## STEP 2:

USING THIS METHOD, WORK YOUR WAY UP YOUR BODY, SQUEEZING AND RELAXING EACH DIFFERENT MUSCLE AS YOU GO. AFTER YOUR TOES, YOU CAN MOVE ON TO YOUR LEGS, STOMACH, SHOULDERS, ARMS, AND HANDS. LASTLY, SCRUNCH UP YOUR FACE AS TIGHT AS YOU CAN FOR A COUNT OF FOUR AND THEN RELAX IT. WE HOLD A LOT OF TENSION IN OUR JAWS BECAUSE WE USE THEM ALL THE TIME FOR THINGS LIKE EATING AND TALKING. RELAXING YOUR JAW CAN STOP YOU FROM GETTING HEADACHES.

**BUDDHISTS** BELIEVE THAT TAKING TIME TO RELAX AND FOCUSING ON YOUR BREATHING CAN HELP YOU CLEAR YOUR MIND OF WORRYING THOUGHTS. THIS IS CALLED MEDITATION.

# Visualization

When we are anxious, our brains tend to look for things that prove that we need to be scared. For example, if you were worried that your friend didn't like you, you might see every whisper or giggle in a **NEGATIVE** way and think they were talking about you, even though they probably weren't. One way to understand how your brain works when you're anxious is to practice the following technique:

Start by closing your eyes and **VISUALIZING** the room around you. While your eyes are closed, try to remember all of the objects in the room that are red. How many can you think of? When you open your eyes again, take a good look around the room. Can you see some red objects you didn't think of before? You might find you can't stop seeing red things.

This is a bit like what happens in your mind when you have anxiety. When you are feeling anxious about something, it can feel like everything around you reminds you of that worry.

ONCE YOU KNOW YOU ARE TOO FOCUSED ON A PROBLEM, YOU CAN CHANGE THE WAY YOU THINK ABOUT IT. FIND OUT MORE ABOUT THIS ON PAGE 27.

# DIFFERENT FEARS

There are two types of fears: rational fears and irrational fears. Rational fears are about things that are likely to happen and are in your control. It makes sense to worry about remembering your lines in a school play. This type of worry will motivate you to practice your lines so you remember them on the night. Irrational fears are about things that are less likely to happen and are out of your control.

For example, being scared of being struck by lightning would be considered an irrational fear because, although it is frightening, it is very unlikely to happen and it is completely out of your control.

IF SOMEONE WAS SO FRIGHTENED OF BEING STRUCK BY LIGHTNING THAT THEY AVOIDED EVER GOING OUTSIDE IN BAD WEATHER, IT MIGHT BE CONSIDERED A PHOBIA.

Everybody has a mixture of both rational and irrational fears, but people with anxiety are more likely to have irrational fears. However, people with anxiety can also worry **EXCESSIVELY** about rational fears. Everybody has different fears and everyone's fears are important. No matter how silly somebody's fear feels to you, it is very real and frightening to them. We should always try to be understanding and treat everybody's rational and irrational fears with equal amounts of understanding.

When dealing with rational fears, we can try to come up with ways that we can solve our problems. For example, if you are worried about an upcoming test, you can solve the problem by talking to a teacher about how you feel. However, sometimes we have no control over the things we are worried about. This can feel very scary, but it won't always feel this way. After telling someone how you are feeling, they can help you come to terms with these sorts of fears.

SOMETIMES ASKING OURSELVES "WHAT'S THE WORST THING THAT COULD HAPPEN?" CAN HELP US TO FACE OUR FEARS, AND OFTEN THE WORST THING THAT COULD HAPPEN ISN'T AS SCARY AS WE FIRST THOUGHT.

# JOSIE

My name is Josie and I see a counselor for my anxiety disorder. I didn't know what anxiety was before and people used to just call me a "worrywart." I didn't like this because it made my fears seem silly even when they were really frightening. My biggest worry was about getting sick or having a terrible disease. My mom's friend was told she had cancer and I was really frightened that I would get cancer too or that my mom would get it. Mom told me that cancer was not **CONTAGIOUS**, but I was still worried. I didn't like going to school because I was so far away from my mom. What if she got sick while I wasn't there?

I was always frightened if I felt sick or had a headache at school. What if it was a sign that I had what Mom's friend had? I kept asking to see the school nurse, who told me that my headaches were nothing to worry about, but I didn't believe her.

The next time I went to see the school nurse, she asked me what was bothering me. I told her all about Mom's friend and how scared I was about getting sick like her. She helped me calm down and even helped me talk to my mom about how I was feeling.

Since then I've been seeing a counselor. His name is Chris and he told me that my headaches are a symptom of anxiety and not cancer or any other illness. He also told me that anxiety can make you concentrate too closely on little aches and pains and this can make them feel stronger.

Chris thought I might be scared because I didn't really understand what was happening to Mom's friend, so he taught me more about what cancer is and all the ways that doctors treat it. This scared me at first, but Chris was there for me when I got upset. Now that I know more about it, I'm not as frightened. I don't think my anxiety has completely gone away, but I know that with Chris's help I can fight it.

# THOUGHT TRAPS

Anxiety causes people to have lots of negative thoughts, which can make them feel even worse. For example, we might find ourselves always expecting the **WORST-CASE SCENARIO**, or always blaming ourselves for things that go wrong. These negative thought patterns are called thought traps because it is easy to get caught in these ways of thinking.

## CATASTROPHIZING

ALWAYS EXPECTING THE WORST IS A COMMON THOUGHT TRAP CALLED CATASTROPHIZING (SAY: CAT-AS-TRO-FYE-ZING). CATASTROPHIZING CAN AFFECT THE WAY WE BEHAVE. FOR EXAMPLE, IF YOU WANTED TO TAKE PART IN THE SCHOOL PLAY BUT WERE TOO SCARED TO AUDITION BECAUSE YOU IMAGINED FORGETTING ALL YOUR LINES ON THE NIGHT, THIS WOULD MEAN YOU NEVER GOT THE OPPORTUNITY TO DO WHAT YOU WANTED.

## ALL-OR-NOTHING THINKING

ANOTHER THOUGHT TRAP IS CALLED ALL-OR-NOTHING THINKING. AN EXAMPLE OF ALL-OR-NOTHING THINKING WOULD BE THINKING YOU ARE A FAILURE BECAUSE YOU FORGOT TO DO YOUR HOMEWORK. THIS IS AN ALL-OR-NOTHING THOUGHT BECAUSE YOU ARE ASSUMING THAT, IF YOU ARE NOT A PERFECT STUDENT, YOU MUST BE A FAILURE.

NOBODY IS A FAILURE AND NOBODY IS PERFECT EITHER. WE ALL MAKE MISTAKES; THIS MAKES US HUMAN.

# Catch, Check, and Change

When we fall into a thought trap or have a worrying thought, it is important to remember the three C's: catch, check, and change. We start by catching the thought and examining it rather than simply accepting it. Next, we can check the thought and weigh up how it actually is. Where is the evidence that this thought is true? Lastly, we can change the thought to something more positive. By reminding ourselves to catch, check, and change our thoughts, we can start to challenge our anxiety.

**CATCH**

My friends don't want to hang out with me. They think I'm annoying.

**CHANGE**

I'm a nice person and my friends enjoy spending time with me.

**CHECK**

My friends still ask me to spend time with them. They wouldn't do that if they didn't like me.

# COGNITIVE BEHAVIORAL
# THERAPY (CBT)

There are many different ways of treating anxiety, from learning relaxation techniques to talking about your feelings with a therapist. One of the most common treatments is something called CBT, which stands for cognitive behavioral therapy. This might sound very serious at first, but it is simply a type of therapy that helps people to break the cycle of thoughts and behaviors that feed anxiety.

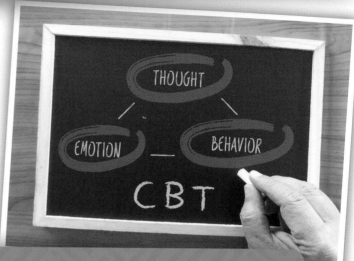

A therapist who is using CBT to treat someone with anxiety might use methods like the catch, check, and change method to help them challenge some of their anxious thoughts and behaviors. Anxiety often makes people avoid things and situations because they believe something bad will happen. However, this means they often don't get to do the things they enjoy and they may never get to prove to themselves that nothing bad will happen. CBT helps people feel strong enough to face situations that they haven't been able to before.

"COGNITIVE" MEANS THOUGHT PROCESSES IN THE MIND.

# ANXIOUS BRAINS

## DO MORE OF WHAT YOU LOVE

Doing more of the things you enjoy can help you to feel better and can provide a good distraction from anxiety. Whether it's playing video games, hanging out with friends, reading, or playing a sport, our hobbies are very important in keeping our minds healthy. Being active is also a great way of keeping our minds and bodies healthy. When we exercise, chemicals called endorphins are released in the brain which help us to concentrate more, feel happier, and even sleep better!

### Use a Scale of One to Ten

When you are feeling anxious, it can often be hard to put your thoughts into words. It can help to tell someone you trust how you feel on a scale of one to ten; ten being the most anxious you've ever been and one being really relaxed. You can then simply say, "I'm feeling about a seven" or even just hold up seven fingers. You can even do this in your own head and focus on using the relaxation techniques from earlier in this book to bring those numbers down.

# TALKING TO SOMEONE

Because we are not all scared of the same things, it can be hard for people to know you are feeling anxious unless you tell them. Physical illnesses, like chicken pox, have visible symptoms, like spots or a rash. Mental health conditions, like anxiety, often have no visible signs that suggest you are not OK. Our mental health is just as important as our physical health. After all, the brain is a very important part of the body. Talking about how we are feeling is very important for our mental health.

There are lots of people you can talk to about mental health problems like anxiety. You can talk to someone close to you, like a parent, carer, or friend, or a **PROFESSIONAL** like a teacher, doctor, or counselor. Anxiety can make you feel like you are alone and that nobody else worries about the things you do, but that's not true. No matter how strange, embarrassing, or complicated you think your fears are, it is always better to share them with someone else so they can help you feel better.

# GLOSSARY

| | |
|---|---|
| ANCESTORS | people from whom one is descended, for example a great-grandparent |
| BUDDHISTS | people who follow the philosophy of Buddhism |
| CHEMICAL IMBALANCES | having too much or not enough of certain chemicals in the brain |
| CONTAGIOUS | (of a disease) able to spread from one person to another |
| EXCESSIVELY | to an amount that is more than what is wanted or needed |
| EVOLVED | gradually developed over a long time |
| FREQUENT | occurring often |
| GLANDS | organs in the body that produce chemical substances for the body to use or get rid of |
| HORMONE | a chemical in your body that tells cells what to do |
| INTENSE | to a strong degree |
| NAUSEA | a sick feeling in the stomach |
| NEGATIVE | not helpful or constructive |
| PALPITATIONS | noticeably rapid, strong, or irregular heartbeats |
| PHYSICALLY | relating to the body |
| PROFESSIONAL | having to do with a certain job or work |
| SELF-ESTEEM | how someone feels about themselves and their own abilities |
| STRESS | a state of mental or emotional tension |
| SYMPTOMS | things that happen in the body suggesting that there is a disease or disorder |
| THERAPIST | a person who is specially trained to treat mental health conditions |
| TRIGGER | to cause or set off |
| VICIOUS CYCLE | when the response to a problem creates a new problem, which, in turn, feeds into the original difficulty |
| VISUALIZING | vividly imagining |
| WORST-CASE SCENARIO | the worst possible outcome |

# INDEX